S0-CFO-267

Sodium

and the Alkali Metals

Nigel Saunders

Heinemann Library
Chicago, Illinois

LIBRARY
EDWARD LITTLE HIGH SCHOOL

© 2004 Heinemann Library
a division of Reed Elsevier Inc.
Chicago, Illinois

Customer Service 888-454-2279

Visit our website at www.heinemannlibrary.com

All rights reserved. No part of this publication may be reproduced or transmitted in any form or by any means, electronic or mechanical, including photocopying, recording, taping, or any information storage and retrieval system, without permission in writing from the publisher.

Design: Ian Winton
Illustrations: Stefan Chabluk
Picture Research: Vashti Gwynn

Originated by Ambassador Litho, Ltd.
Printed and bound in China by
South China Printing Company

08 0706 05 04
10 9 8 7 6 5 4 3 2 1

Library of Congress Cataloging-in-Publication Data

Saunders, N. (Nigel)
  Sodium and the alkali metals / Nigel Saunders.
    v. cm. -- (The periodic table)
Includes bibliographical references and index.
Contents: Elements and atomic structure -- The periodic table, sodium, and the alkali metals -- Trends in group 1 -- Lithium -- Sodium -- Potassium -- Rubidium -- Caesium -- Francium -- Find out more.
  ISBN 1-4034-1665-6 (HC), 1-4034-5499-X (Pbk.)
  1. Sodium--Juvenile literature. 2. Alkali metals--Juvenile literature. [1. Sodium. 2. Alkali metals. 3. Metals. 4. Chemical elements.] I. Title. II. Series.
  QD181.N2S28 2003
  546'.38--dc21

                              2003010228

Acknowledgments

The publishers would like to thank the following for permission to reproduce photographs:
p. 1 Discovery Books Picture Library; p. 8 Dex Images/Corbis; p. 9 Francoise Sauze/Science Photo library; p. 10 Corbis; p. 11 L. Clarke/Corbis; p. 12 Jerry Mason/Science Photo Library; p. 13 Jerry Mason/Science Photo Library; p. 15 Ron Watts/Corbis; p. 17 Charles D Winters/Science Photo Library; p. 20 Sheila Terry/Science Photo Library; p. 22 Discovery Books Picture Library; p. 23 Discovery Books Picture Library; p. 25 Hotpoint; p. 27 R. Maisonneuve, Publiphoto Diffusion/Science Photo Library; p. 28 Martyn F Chillmaid/Science Photo Library; p. 29 Paul A. Souders/Corbis; p. 31 Roger Ressmeyer/Corbis; p. 32 Science Picture Limited/Corbis; p. 33 Discovery Books Picture Library; p. 35 George Shelley, Inc./Corbis; p. 36 John Greim/Science Photo Library; p. 40 Buddy Mays/Corbis; p. 41 Doug Wilson/Corbis; p. 42 Sinclair Stammers/ Science Photo Library; p. 45 Adam Hart-Davis/ Corbis; p. 45 Adam Hart-Davis/Science Photo Library; p. 46 Quest/Science Photo Library; p. 47 Tom Stewart/Corbis; p. 49 Neal Preston/ Corbis; p. 50 Alexandra Tsiaris/Science Photo Library; p. 52 Alexandra Tsiaris/Science Photo Library; p. 54 Chris Priest/Science Photo Library; p. 55 CRDPHOTO/Corbis; p. 56 American Institute of Physics/Science Photo Library; p. 57 Fermilab/Science Photo Library; p. 58 James L. Amos, Peter Arnold Inc./Science Photo Library

Cover photograph of salt crystals reproduced with permission of Corbis.

Special thanks to Theodore Dolter for his review of this book.

The author would like to thank Angela, Kathryn, David, and Jean for all their help and support.

Every effort has been made to contact copyright holders of any material reproduced in this book. A omissions will be rectified in subsequent printings notice is given to the publishers.

Disclaimer

All the Internet addresses (URLs) given in this book were valid at the time of going to press. However, due to the dynamic nature of the Internet, some addresses may have changed, or sites may have ceased to exist since publication. While the author and publishers regret any inconvenience this may cause readers, no responsibility for any such changes can be accepted by either author or the publishers.

31198000128135

Contents

Elements and Atomic Structure

There are millions of different substances around us. Some of them are gases, such as air; others are liquids, such as water; but most of them are solids, like this book. They do have one thing in common however: they are all made from just a few simple substances called elements.

Everything you can see here, including the train, cars, and buildings, is made from some of the millions of substances in the world. Some of the substances, such as the oxygen in the air, are elements, but most are compounds.

Elements and compounds

Elements are substances that cannot be broken down into anything simpler by using chemical reactions. About 90 elements occur naturally, and scientists have learned how to make more than 20 more using nuclear reactions. Approximately three-quarters of the elements are metals, such as sodium. The rest are nonmetals, such as chlorine. Elements can join together in countless different ways in chemical reactions to make compounds. An example of this is when sodium and chlorine react together to make the compound sodium chloride, which is table salt. Most of the millions of different substances in the world are compounds, made up of two or more elements chemically bonded together.

Atoms

Every substance, whether it is an element or a compound, is made up of tiny particles called atoms. An element contains just one type of atom, whereas compounds are made from two or more different types of atom joined together. Although we can see most of the substances around us, individual atoms are far too tiny for us to see, even with a microscope. Francium atoms are the biggest of the alkali metals, but even if you could stack a million of them on top of one another, the pile would be only about half a millimeter high!

Subatomic particles

Scientists used to think that atoms were the smallest things in the universe. However, they now know that atoms consist of even smaller objects called subatomic particles. The biggest subatomic particles, called protons and neutrons, are joined together in the center of the atom to form a nucleus. Electrons are subatomic particles that are even smaller than protons and neutrons. They are arranged around the nucleus in different shells, or energy levels.

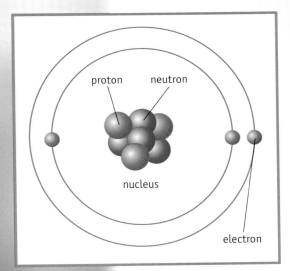

◀ *This is a model of a lithium atom. Each lithium atom contains three protons and four neutrons, with three electrons arranged in two shells, or energy levels, around the nucleus.*

Groups

Chemistry is exciting and unpredictable because the elements all react in different ways. Several attempts were made to sort the elements to make things more predictable, but it was a Russian chemist named Dimitri Mendeleev who was the most successful. In 1869 he made a table in which each element was placed into one of eight groups, with similar elements in each group. This made it much easier for chemists to predict the properties of the elements. Mendeleev's table was so successful that the modern periodic table developed from it.

The Periodic Table, Sodium, and the Alkali Metals

The modern periodic table shown here is based closely on Mendeleev's table. The elements are arranged in horizontal rows called periods, with the atomic number (number of protons in the nucleus) increasing from left to right. Each vertical column in the periodic table is called a group, and the elements in each group have similar chemical properties. There are eighteen groups altogether.

Elements in a group all have the same number of electrons in the shell farthest from the nucleus, called the outer shell. For example, the elements in group 2 are all metals with two electrons in their outer shells, whereas the elements in group 7 are nonmetals with seven electrons in their outer shells. The elements in both groups react quickly with other substances. The periodic table gets its name because the elements are arranged so that their different chemical properties recur regularly, or periodically.

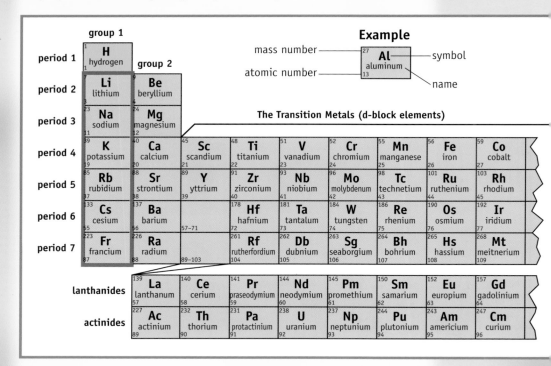

The properties of the elements change gradually as you go down a group. For example, in group 18 the elements become denser. Balloons filled with helium (at the top of the group) rise quickly into the air, which is why they are such fun at parties. Balloons filled with argon (from the middle of the group) fall slowly. However, balloons filled with xenon (near the bottom of the group) fall to the ground quickly.

Sodium and the alkali metals

The elements in group 1 are all metals. They are often called the alkali metals because they produce alkalis when they react with water. They are usually too soft and reactive for anything to be built out of them, but their compounds are useful to us in many ways. In this book you will find out all about sodium and the other alkali metals and many of their uses.

▼ This is the periodic table of the elements. Group 1 contains lithium, sodium, potassium, rubidium, cesium, and francium, which are all metals.

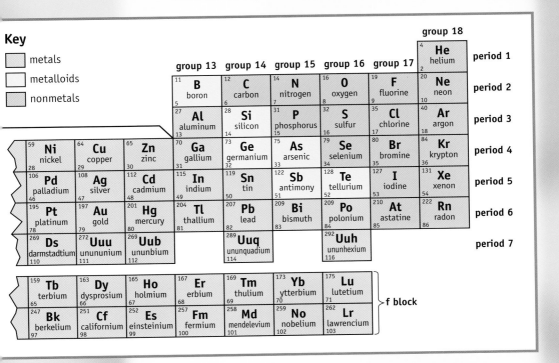

Key

▢ metals
▢ metalloids
▢ nonmetals

group 18

							4 **He** helium 2	period 1
		group 13	group 14	group 15	group 16	group 17	20 **Ne** neon 10	period 2
		11 **B** boron 5	12 **C** carbon 6	14 **N** nitrogen 7	16 **O** oxygen 8	19 **F** fluorine 9		
		27 **Al** aluminum 13	28 **Si** silicon 14	31 **P** phosphorus 15	32 **S** sulfur 16	35 **Cl** chlorine 17	40 **Ar** argon 18	period 3
59 **Ni** nickel 28	64 **Cu** copper 29	65 **Zn** zinc 30	70 **Ga** gallium 31	73 **Ge** germanium 32	75 **As** arsenic 33	79 **Se** selenium 34	80 **Br** bromine 35	84 **Kr** krypton 36	period 4
106 **Pd** palladium 46	108 **Ag** silver 47	112 **Cd** cadmium 48	115 **In** indium 49	119 **Sn** tin 50	122 **Sb** antimony 51	128 **Te** tellurium 52	127 **I** iodine 53	131 **Xe** xenon 54	period 5
195 **Pt** platinum 78	197 **Au** gold 79	201 **Hg** mercury 80	204 **Tl** thallium 81	207 **Pb** lead 82	209 **Bi** bismuth 83	209 **Po** polonium 84	210 **At** astatine 85	222 **Rn** radon 86	period 6
269 **Ds** darmstadtium 110	272 **Uuu** unununium 111	269 **Uub** ununbium 112		289 **Uuq** ununquadium 114		292 **Uuh** ununhexium 116			period 7

159 **Tb** terbium 65	163 **Dy** dysprosium 66	165 **Ho** holmium 67	167 **Er** erbium 68	169 **Tm** thulium 69	173 **Yb** ytterbium 70	175 **Lu** lutetium 71	f block
247 **Bk** berkelium 97	251 **Cf** californium 98	252 **Es** einsteinium 99	257 **Fm** fermium 100	258 **Md** mendelevium 101	259 **No** nobelium 102	262 **Lr** lawrencium 103	

Introducing the Elements of Group 1

There are six elements in group 1. They are lithium, sodium, potassium, rubidium, cesium, and francium (as you move down the group). They are fairly soft, silvery-white metals and they all react with water to make alkaline solutions. They are all solids at room temperature. However, the melting points of rubidium and cesium are low enough for them to become liquids on very hot days.

7	Li	**lithium**
	lithium	symbol: Li • atomic number: 3 • metal
3		

What does it look like? Lithium is soft enough to be cut fairly easily with a steel knife. At first, the cut surface is shiny but it quickly becomes dull. This is because the exposed metal reacts with oxygen in the air to form lithium oxide. This is why pieces of lithium often look grey. Lithium is usually stored in oil to stop the element from reacting with water and oxygen in the air.

Where is it found? Lithium is too reactive to be found naturally as a pure metal. Instead, it is found all over the world as various compounds in minerals such as spodumene and lepidolite.

What are its main uses? Lithium is mixed with other metals to make alloys. These are used by the aircraft industry and for batteries for laptop computers. Lithium compounds have many uses, including cosmetics, heat-resistant cookwear, and devices called scrubbers, that keep the air supply safe for astronauts to breathe.

Batteries containing lithium are used in many electronic devices, including watches, cell phones, and laptop computers. ▶

23		**sodium**
Na		symbol: Na • atomic number: 11 • metal
sodium		
11		

What does it look like?   Just like lithium, sodium can be cut easily with a knife, revealing a shiny surface. Within seconds, the surface reacts with oxygen in the air to form a dull layer of sodium oxide, making it appear light grey. Sodium is normally stored in oil to block any reactions with water and oxygen in the air.

Where is it found?   Sodium is the sixth most abundant element in the earth's crust and it is found, as a compound, in many minerals, including borax (sodium borate) and Chile saltpetre (sodium nitrate). The most common sodium mineral is rock salt (sodium chloride). The oceans contain vast quantities of sodium chloride. This is the main compound that makes the sea salty.

▼ *These salt pans in France produce 3,000 tons of salt (sodium chloride) a year. The salt is left behind as water evaporates from the shallow pools of seawater.*

What are its main uses?   Sodium is used in nuclear power stations and to **extract** titanium metal. Sodium chloride is used as table salt and to make other compounds that are important for the manufacture of many familiar things, including glass, paper, plastics, and detergents.

More Elements of Group 1

39	
K	
potassium	
19	

potassium

symbol: K • atomic number: 19 • metal

What does it look like?   Even though the metal is silvery, pieces of potassium often look dark gray because they are covered by potassium oxide. Potassium is soft enough to be molded using finger pressure. To prevent it from reacting with air and water, it is usually stored in oil.

Where is it found?   Potassium is the eighth most abundant element in the earth's crust, but because it is so reactive it is found only as a compound. It is present in many minerals, including potash (potassium hydroxide) and sylvite (potassium chloride). The sea also contains a lot of potassium compounds.

What are its main uses?   Potassium compounds are widely used in fertilizers to help crops grow properly and in explosives for fireworks and mining.

85	
Rb	
rubidium	
37	

rubidium

symbol: Rb • atomic number: 37 • metal

What does it look like?   Rubidium is a very soft, silvery metal. In very hot weather, rubidium may become a liquid because it melts at only 39 °C (102 °F). It is usually stored in an unreactive gas such as argon because rubidium would react with just about everything else.

Where is it found?   Rubidium is not found naturally as a pure metal because of its reactivity. Several minerals contain tiny amounts of rubidium compounds, but it is much rarer than lithium, sodium, or potassium. Rubidium is usually obtained from the waste material produced when lithium is extracted from lepidolite.

What are its main uses?   Rubidium is used in photoelectric cells and in electronic devices called vacuum tubes.

133		**cesium**
Cs		symbol: Cs • atomic number: 55 • metal
cesium		
55		

What does it look like?   Cesium (pronounced *see-zee-um*) is a very soft metal with a very faint gold color. It is very reactive and must be stored in a vacuum or an unreactive gas such as argon. Cesium melts at 28 °C (82 °F), and your body heat is enough to melt it if you held its container.

Where is it found?   The metallic form of cesium is not found naturally, and it is even rarer than rubidium. A mineral called pollucite contains cesium aluminum silicate, but cesium is usually extracted from the materials left over when lithium is obtained from lepidolite.

What are its main uses?   Cesium is used in atomic clocks, which are incredibly accurate and are used to keep clocks all over the world in step with one another. Radioactive cesium is used to treat cancer.

◀ *Potassium nitrate is an ingredient of gunpowder, which is used in spectacular fireworks like these.*

223		**francium**
Fr		symbol: Fr • atomic number: 87 • metal
francium		
87		

What does it look like?   Francium is highly radioactive, and no one has actually seen enough of it to know what it looks like. However, chemists expect it to be a very soft, silvery metal—just like the other alkali metals.

Where is it found?   Francium is incredibly rare. There are probably only a few grams of it in the earth's crust at any one time! If scientists want to study francium, they make it using nuclear reactions.

What are its main uses?   Francium has no commercial uses, but research scientists study it to see if their predictions about its properties are accurate.

Trends in Group 1

The alkali metals react with oxygen, water, and dilute acid in similar ways. However, the reactions are not identical because these metals become more reactive from top to bottom on the periodic table. A gradual change in a property such as reactivity is called a trend. Lithium, at the top of the group, is the least reactive; potassium, near the middle, is more reactive than lithium; and francium, at the bottom, is the most reactive. But it is almost impossible to study the chemistry of francium because it is radioactive and very rare.

Reactions with acids

All the alkali metals react with acids to produce metal salts and hydrogen gas, H_2. The salt formed depends upon the metal and acid used. For example, if sodium reacts with hydrochloric acid, HCl, it makes sodium chloride, NaCl.

The equation for the reaction of sodium with hydrochloric acid is:

sodium + hydrochloric acid ➞ sodium chloride + hydrogen

$$2Na + 2HCl \longrightarrow 2NaCl + H_2$$

If sodium reacts with sulphuric acid, H_2SO_4, it makes sodium sulphate, Na_2SO_4.

The equation for the reaction of sodium with sulphuric acid is:

sodium + sulphuric acid ➞ sodium sulphate + hydrogen

$$2Na + H_2SO_4 \longrightarrow Na_2SO_4 + H_2$$

Reactions with oxygen

All the alkali metals react with oxygen to form metal oxides. For example, sodium reacts with oxygen to produce sodium oxide, Na_2O, and potassium reacts with oxygen to produce potassium oxide, K_2O.

This is molten sodium metal burning in oxygen. The reaction between sodium and oxygen is very vigorous, producing a bright flame and clouds of white sodium oxide. ▶

When lithium is heated in air, it ignites with a small white flame. Sodium, on the other hand, burns with an orange flame. If burning lithium or sodium is lowered into a jar of pure oxygen gas, they both burn more brightly and produce clouds of white lithium oxide or sodium oxide.

> *The equation for the reaction of sodium with oxygen is*
>
> sodium + oxygen → sodium oxide
>
> $$4Na + O_2 \rightarrow 2Na_2O$$
>
> *This type of reaction is called a synthesis reaction because a compound is made by chemically combining its elements.*

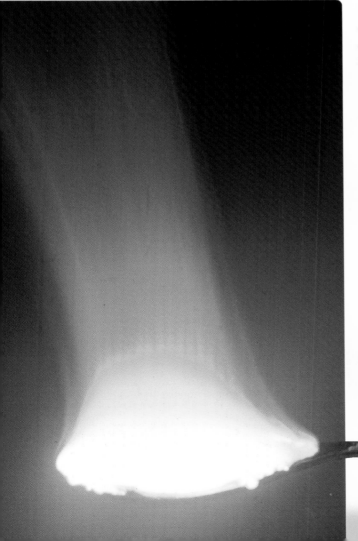

Potassium burns in air with a lilac-colored flame. When lowered into a jar of pure oxygen, the potassium burns more quickly and the flame becomes so hot that it turns white, producing clouds of white potassium oxide, K_2O. Rubidium and cesium are even more reactive than potassium. They ignite and react with the oxygen in the air without being heated first. Rubidium produces brown rubidium superoxide, RbO_2, and cesium produces orange-red cesium superoxide, CsO_2.

Colorful Chemistry

Each salt of the alkali metals produces its own characteristic color when it is put into a flame. If some table salt is sprinkled into a Bunsen burner flame, the sodium in the salt turns the flame bright orange. The flame color depends upon the metal in the salt, and chemists can use these flame tests to determine which metal is in an unknown salt.

Flame tests

A loop of platinum wire is used in flame tests. For a good result it must be really clean, so it is immersed into concentrated nitric acid and rinsed in distilled water. The loop is then dipped into the salt or its solution and held in the hottest part of the Bunsen burner flame. The flame changes color depending upon the metal in the salt.

Excited, but not for long

When energy, such as heat, is applied to an atom, its electrons become excited and jump into a shell farther from the nucleus. Electrons cannot stay in this excited state for long, and they fall back to a shell closer to the nucleus, emitting their extra energy as light. Long falls produce blue light and short falls red light. Each element forms a unique spectrum of colors because its electrons make different jumps and falls.

▼ Electrons can jump into another shell if they are given the right amount of energy. When they fall back to their normal shell, they give out this energy as light.

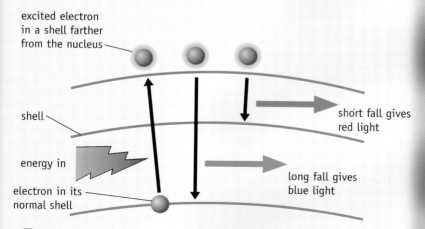

excited electron in a shell farther from the nucleus

shell

energy in

electron in its normal shell

short fall gives red light

long fall gives blue light

All the colors of the rainbow

White light has a spectrum that is made up of all the colors. These are red, orange, yellow, green, blue, indigo, and violet. Prisms split light up so that its spectrum is displayed. A device called a spectroscope is used to study the light given out during a flame test. Simple spectroscopes contain a prism to split the light into its spectrum. Gustav Kirchhoff was the first person to realize that every element produces a different spectrum.

Two German scientists, Gustav Kirchhoff and Robert Bunsen, used a spectroscope to study the light emitted in flame tests. They discovered cesium in 1860 and rubidium in 1861 as a result. A new type of burner provided the very hot flame needed for their experiments. Although called the Bunsen burner, it was actually designed and built by Peter Desaga, a technician at the University of Heidelberg, where Bunsen worked.

Street lamps

Heat is not the only form of energy that can cause atoms to emit light. Gases trapped inside tubes at below normal pressure will glow if electricity is passed through them. Fluorescent lights and neon lights work like this. Sodium street lamps produce orange light because electricity is passed through sodium vapor. Neon gas is used to start up these lamps so they make a red glow when they are first switched on. As the lamp warms up, sodium metal is vaporized and the light turns orange.

▲
Sodium lamps produce more light for the same amount of electrical energy than many ordinary light bulbs. They are often used to light streets and highways at night.

Reactions with Water

All the alkali metals react with water to produce a metal hydroxide and hydrogen gas. For example, sodium reacts with water to produce sodium hydroxide, NaOH.

> *The equation for sodium reacting with water is*
>
> sodium + water $\rightarrow$ sodium hydroxide + hydrogen
>
> $2Na + 2H_2O \rightarrow 2NaOH + H_2$

The metal hydroxides are white solids that dissolve easily in water, making the water alkaline. However, the reactions become more dangerous as you go from lithium, at the top of the group, to cesium, at the bottom.

Lithium

When lithium is dropped into water, it fizzes and floats on the surface. It gradually becomes smaller until it eventually disappears. The lithium does not vanish; it reacts with the water to produce soluble lithium hydroxide. Universal indicator is a mixture of dyes used to tell if a substance is acidic, alkaline, or neutral. It turns purple when added to the water, showing that the lithium hydroxide solution is alkaline. The fizzing is caused by the hydrogen gas made in the reaction. This can be ignited and although hydrogen normally burns with a colorless flame, it has a red color because some lithium atoms are present.

Sodium

So much heat is produced by the reaction when sodium is dropped into water that it melts into a shiny ball. This ball whizzes around, producing many bubbles of hydrogen gas and leaving a trail of white sodium hydroxide. Eventually it disappears with a small popping sound. The sodium hydroxide dissolves into the water, making it alkaline. If a few drops of water are dropped onto a piece of sodium, the heat builds up until the sodium catches fire with an orange flame and a lot of smoke.

This is potassium reacting with drops of water to make potassium hydroxide and hydrogen gas. The hydrogen burns with a flame colored lilac by vaporized potassium.

Potassium

The reaction of potassium and water is very fast. When water is dripped onto potassium, the potassium ignites right away with a lilac flame and sparks. If a small piece of potassium is added to water, it floats and immediately catches fire. Sometimes it explodes. The metal disappears within a few seconds, and the reaction produces potassium hydroxide and hydrogen gas.

Rubidium

Rubidium and water react extremely fast. As soon as the rubidium touches the surface of the water, it explodes in a shower of sparks and red flames, producing rubidium hydroxide and hydrogen. Molten pieces of rubidium may shoot out of the water. This reaction is seldom demonstrated in schools because it is so dangerous.

Cesium and francium

When cesium reacts with water, it is incredibly hazardous. After being dropped into water, cesium sinks, producing many hydrogen bubbles. It then explodes violently, producing cesium hydroxide and hydrogen. Cesium is so reactive that it even reacts with ice at −100 °C (−148 °F)! Because francium is so rare, it is unlikely that anyone has ever investigated how it reacts with water, but chemists expect it to be even more dangerous than cesium.

What Causes the Reactivity Trend?

The electrons in an atom are arranged in shells around its nucleus. The outer shell is the farthest from the nucleus and the most important one for chemists. In most cases the outer shell is completely full when it contains eight electrons. Atoms with full outer shells, such as helium, neon, and the other noble gases in group 18, are stable and unreactive.

The outer shells of the other elements are not completely filled with electrons. These atoms react with others to fill them up. In a chemical reaction between a metal, such as sodium, and a nonmetal, such as chlorine, the atoms fill their outer shells by passing electrons from one to the other. The compound formed, sodium chloride, is stable and unreactive.

Electrons hold the key

Metal atoms have unfilled outer shells, often containing only one, two, or three electrons. They give these electrons to other atoms during chemical reactions, and the full shell underneath becomes their new outer shell. In contrast, nonmetal atoms have outer shells that are usually just one, two, or three electrons short of being full. It is simpler for nonmetal atoms to receive electrons from other atoms to complete their outer shells.

The alkali metals have atoms with only one electron in their outer shell. During a reaction with nonmetals, these single electrons are transferred to the nonmetal atoms. The easier it is to transfer the electron, the more reactive the alkali metal.

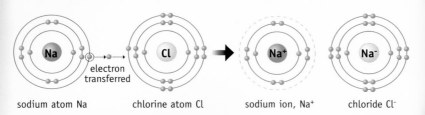

sodium atom Na   chlorine atom Cl   sodium ion, Na⁺   chloride Cl⁻

When sodium reacts with chlorine, each sodium atom transfers its outer electron to a chlorine atom. This produces electrically charged particles called ions, which are attracted to one another and form strong chemical bonds.

Transfer those electrons

Lithium atoms are the smallest in group 1 and not very reactive. The electron in the outer shell is close to the nucleus of the atom and is very strongly attracted to it. This makes the transfer of an electron to a nonmetal atom relatively difficult. Moving down group 1, the atoms become larger and correspondingly more reactive. As the distance between the electron and the nucleus increases, the attraction between them lessens. As a result, it is easier for the electron to be transferred during reactions. Francium, at the bottom of the group, has the largest atoms and should be the most reactive. However, its rarity and radioactivity makes it difficult to study.

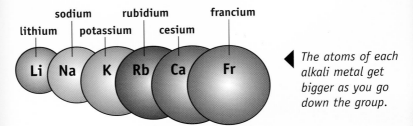

sodium   rubidium   francium

lithium   potassium   cesium

Li   Na   K   Rb   Ca   Fr

◀ The atoms of each alkali metal get bigger as you go down the group.

The reactivity series

If metals are listed in order of their reactivity, with the most reactive metal first, the list is called a reactivity series. Chemists can make a long reactivity series by studying the reactions of other metals, not just the alkali metals. By looking at a metal's position in the series, they can predict how it should react.

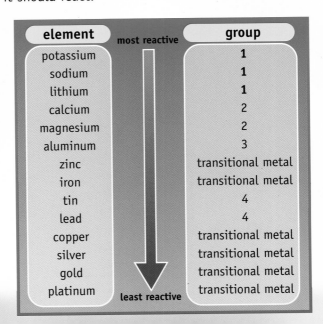

element		group
potassium	most reactive	1
sodium		1
lithium		1
calcium		2
magnesium		2
aluminum		3
zinc		transitional metal
iron		transitional metal
tin		4
lead		4
copper		transitional metal
silver		transitional metal
gold		transitional metal
platinum	least reactive	transitional metal

Lithium

Lithium is a soft, silvery metal that reacts quickly with air and water. Storing it in oil stops this from happening.

The discovery of lithium

Johan Arfwedson, a Swedish chemist, discovered lithium in 1817. Arfwedson was studying a mineral called petalite to search for potassium compounds, but the compounds he extracted from the petalite had different properties from those he expected. He was sure that he had discovered a new element, which he named lithium from the Greek word for "stone." Unfortunately he was only able to isolate some lithium compounds, not the metal itself. A year later, an English chemist named Sir Humphry Davy used a process called electrolysis to isolate lithium metal.

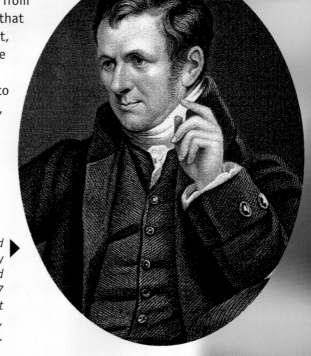

Sir Humphry Davy isolated lithium metal using electricity in 1818. He also discovered sodium and potassium in 1807 and in 1808 became the first person to isolate magnesium, calcium, strontium, and barium.

Lithium minerals

Lithium is rare in the Earth's crust. On average, each ton of rock contains only about 20 grams (0.7 ounces) of it. However, several minerals contain lithium compounds in large enough amounts to make them worth mining. These minerals include petalite, spodumene, lepidolite, and amblygonite, which are all complex compounds. Chile is the biggest single producer of lithium ores, but China and Australia are also major producers. Around 40,000 tons of lithium are used in the world each year, mostly as lithium compounds rather than the metal itself.

Extracting lithium

Several steps are needed to extract lithium from its ores. The ore is crushed, heated strongly, and then mixed with sulfuric acid. A solution of lithium sulfate is produced and filtered to remove impurities. Sodium carbonate is added to the filtered lithium sulfate solution, and solid lithium carbonate is formed. The lithium carbonate is dried, then sold to chemical companies so that they can produce other lithium compounds.

Lithium metal is produced from lithium chloride by electrolysis. The lithium chloride is melted and electricity passed through it. Lithium is formed at the negative electrode, and chlorine gas is produced at the positive electrode.

Electrolysis

Electrolysis is a process that chemists use to split compounds into simpler substances, usually the elements they contain. The compound is first melted or dissolved in water and then an electric current is passed through it between two electrodes—metal or graphite rods that conduct electricity. When the electrodes are dipped into the compound, metals usually form at the negative electrode and nonmetals form at the positive electrode. During the electrolysis of molten lithium oxide, lithium forms at the negative electrode and oxygen at the positive electrode. Sir Humphry Davy used this method to isolate lithium, sodium, and many other metals from their compounds.

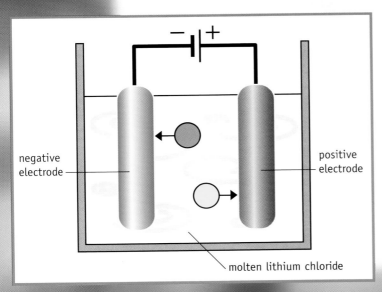

negative electrode

positive electrode

molten lithium chloride

During electrolysis of molten lithium chloride, positively charged lithium ions are attracted to the negative electrode and become lithium atoms. Chloride ions are attracted to the positive electrode and form chlorine gas.

Uses of Lithium

Lithium is more reactive than many other metals, so it is useful for removing unwanted substances, such as oxygen, from brass and copper. Although lithium is too reactive and soft to be used on its own to build things, it can be mixed with other metals to produce alloys with useful properties.

Lithium in space

Aluminum is a metal with a low density, which means that objects made from it are light for their size. The large external fuel tank on the space shuttle was originally made from an aluminum alloy that contained 6 percent copper to give it increased strength. An aluminum alloy containing 1 percent lithium and 4 percent copper is now used to make the external fuel tank.

The space shuttle ▶ Discovery *lifts off from Kennedy Space Center, in Florida. The large brown-colored fuel tank is made from a strong but lightweight aluminum-copper-lithium alloy. Each fuel tank contains 2.5 tons of lithium.*

These new tanks are more than 3 tons lighter than the original tanks and allow the space shuttle to ferry heavier objects into space. Each tank contains around 2.5 tons of lithium. They are the only part of the space shuttle that cannot be reused. When they are empty, they fall back toward Earth and burn up in the atmosphere.

Lithium batteries

Many modern electronic devices need batteries that are lightweight and produce a lot of electricity for their size. Lithium is a useful metal for batteries because it has a low density and is therefore light. It is also a very reactive metal, so it can provide a high voltage.

Electricity and the reactivity series

A simple battery can be made by dipping two different metals into a beaker of weak acid or salty water. Electricity will flow through a wire if it is connected to the dry ends of the metals. The farther apart the two metals are in the reactivity series, the bigger the voltage. A battery made from zinc and copper develops 1.1 volts (V), but one made from lithium and copper could develop three times that much voltage.. Battery designers work hard to design batteries that produce a useful current and are long lasting.

The negative electrode in a lithium battery is made from lithium or a lithium-aluminum alloy. Lithium batteries develop about 3V, twice the voltage of ordinary batteries, and produce electricity for a longer time. Lithium batteries come in a wide variety of sizes, including tiny button batteries used in watches, calculators, and electronic car keys. Larger lithium batteries are used in radios and cameras and as backup power supplies for computer memory chips.

Lithium Carbonate

Some people suffer from an illness called bipolar disorder. This disease causes severe mood swings. Sometimes sufferers are so confident that they take wild and dangerous risks. At other times they become so depressed that they may attempt suicide. Lithium carbonate is the most effective medicine for reducing these symptoms. Lithium carbonate is important in industry as well. About 45,000 tons of it are used each year. Although lithium is often mixed with aluminum to form alloys, lithium carbonate has an important role to play in the extraction of aluminum from bauxite, its ore.

Aluminum production

Aluminum is extracted from bauxite using electrolysis. The bauxite is treated to produce aluminum oxide, which is then melted. When electricity is passed through the molten aluminum oxide, it breaks down to form aluminum at the negative electrode and oxygen at the positive electrode. Unfortunately, a lot of energy is needed to melt the aluminum oxide because it has a high melting point. A mineral called cryolite is used to reduce aluminum oxide's melting point, saving energy and making aluminum cheaper to produce. If lithium carbonate is also added, the melting point of aluminum oxide is reduced even more. This is one of the most common uses for lithium in industry, but it is not the only one.

Cryolite

Aluminum oxide needs to be molten to produce aluminum using electrolysis, but will only melt at temperatures higher than 2000 °C (3600 °F). However aluminum oxide dissolves in cryolite, Na_3AlF_6, a mineral that melts at just over 1000 °C (1800 °F). Like the addition of lithium carbonate, adding cryolite reduces the energy needed to produce molten aluminum oxide, saving a lot of money.

Making glass

Glass is made when sand is melted and then cooled very quickly. However, sand melts at temperatures above 1700 °C (3100 °F)! To reduce the melting temperature to about 800 °C (1500 °F), sodium carbonate is usually added, but lithium carbonate is often added, too. Another advantage of adding lithium carbonate, Li_2CO_3, is that it breaks down in the heat to form lithium oxide, Li_2O, and carbon dioxide, CO_2. Glass containing lithium oxide is stronger than ordinary glass and does not expand as much when it is warmed up. It is used to make heat-resistant glassware for kitchens and laboratories.

▼ *Glass ceramics contain lithium compounds and are used for making missile nose cones, ovenware, and ceramic cooker hobs because they are hardly affected by changes in temperature.*

Lithium carbonate is different

Lithium carbonate is the only alkali metal carbonate that breaks down when heated. Heating sodium carbonate does not cause a chemical reaction. However, heating lithium carbonate causes lithium oxide and carbon dioxide to form:

$$lithium\ carbonate \xrightarrow{\text{heat}} lithium\ oxide + carbon\ dioxide$$

$$Li_2CO_3 \longrightarrow Li_2O + CO_2$$

More Lithium Compounds

The chemical industry uses complex lithium compounds as catalysts for manufacturing medicines, rubber, and plastics, such as polyethylene. Lithium hydroxide is used to make lithium stearate, an ingredient in cosmetics and industrial greases used for cars, aircraft, and ships. Lithium hydroxide has another important use, as a scrubber in submarines and spacecraft.

Scrubbers

Submarines cannot get fresh air underwater, nor can astronauts obtain fresh air in space. A scrubber is a device that recycles the air inside, keeping it safe for the crew to breathe. The simplest scrubbers contain solid lithium hydroxide, which reacts with carbon dioxide, removing it from the air as the crew breathes.

The equation for the reaction between lithium hydroxide and carbon dioxide is

lithium hydroxide + carbon dioxide $\rightarrow$ lithium carbonate + water

$$2LiOH + CO_2 \rightarrow Li_2CO_3 + H_2O$$

Apollo 13

When Apollo 13 got into trouble on the way to the moon in 1970, the crew had to squeeze into the lunar module for the journey back to Earth. To fit the square lithium hydroxide canisters from the command module into the round holes of the lunar module scrubbers, they used sticky tape, cardboard, and plastic bags. If this had not worked, their own carbon dioxide would have killed them.

Some machines in submarines and spacecraft produce small amounts of acidic gases, such as hydrogen chloride. These gases are absorbed by filters containing lithium carbonate.

The equation for the reaction between lithium carbonate and hydrogen chloride is

$$\text{lithium carbonate} + \text{hydrogen chloride} \rightarrow \text{lithium chloride} + \text{water} + \text{carbon dioxide}$$

$$Li_2CO_3 + 2HCl \rightarrow 2LiCl + H_2O + CO_2$$

A foundry worker, wearing protective clothing and goggles, solders copper. The bar of copper is melted with a blow torch and is used to join sheets of metal together. Fluxes containing lithium fluoride help to solder copper and other metals.

Welding and air conditioners

Fluxes are substances that are used when metals are joined by welding, brazing, or soldering. Lithium fluoride is used in fluxes for joining metals such as copper, aluminum, and magnesium. Concentrated solutions of lithium bromide or lithium chloride are used in the large air conditioning machines found in stores, hotels, and hospitals. These liquids are part of the refrigeration equipment that chills the air.

Lithium-ion batteries

Rechargeable lithium-ion batteries are used to power portable electronic equipment such as cell phones, laptop computers, and video cameras. The negative electrodes in lithium-ion batteries are made from complex materials, such as lithium manganese oxide. They release electricity for a longer time than other types of batteries of a similar size, such as nickel-cadmium (NiCd) batteries, and produce 3.6 V. Although they are more expensive, fewer batteries are needed so they can be more economical in some situations.

Sodium

A soft, silvery metal, sodium reacts rapidly with air and water. It is stored in oil to prevent this from happening.

The discovery of sodium
People have known about sodium compounds and used them for thousands of years. However, sodium itself was not discovered until 1807 because in nature it is always combined with other elements. Once Alessandro Volta invented the battery, chemists had the tool they needed to discover reactive metals such as sodium. When Sir Humphry Davy used a battery to pass electricity through molten caustic soda, which we now know is sodium hydroxide, he discovered sodium metal forming at the negative electrode.

▲ *Sodium metal (above) is usually stored in oil to keep it from reacting with air and water.*

The name sodium comes from *sodanum,* the Latin name for a plant called glasswort that grows in salt marshes. The ancient Romans used glasswort to cure headaches. They also burned it to produce ashes that contained sodium carbonate. These ashes were used in glass making. The symbol for sodium, Na, comes from *natrium,* the Latin name for sodium carbonate.

Volta's battery
An Italian scientist named Alessandro Volta invented the first battery in 1799. The electrical term volt *comes from his name. His device, called a voltaic pile, was made from a stack of copper and zinc discs, each separated by a piece of cloth soaked in concentrated salt water. Chemists were eager to see what would happen to different chemicals when electricity was passed through them, and they rushed to build their own batteries. Sir Humphry Davy was particularly successful with his battery, discovering sodium and potassium in 1807. A year later, he became the first person to isolate magnesium, calcium, strontium, and barium.*

Sodium minerals

Only five elements are more plentiful than sodium in the earth's crust. On average, each ton of rock contains more than 20 kilograms (44 pounds) of sodium in various compounds. The most common is sodium chloride, found in rock salt or halite, but sodium is found in other minerals, such as sodalite, cryolite, and sodium nitrate.

Each cubic meter (35 cubic feet) of seawater contains about 26 kilograms (57 pounds) of sodium chloride. This means that the oceans contain an amazing 35,000 trillion tons. If you had been around when Earth formed 4.5 billion years ago and started measuring out a ton of sea salt every four seconds, you would have only recently finished!

▼ *Huge mounds of rock salt, sodium chloride, are piled at the Lake Grassmere salt works, in New Zealand.*

Uses of Sodium

About 70,000 tons of sodium metal are produced in the world each year. It is extracted from rock salt or salt recovered from seawater by evaporation. Apart from being very reactive, sodium has other useful properties and some surprising uses.

Extraction of sodium

Sodium is extracted from sodium chloride using electrolysis in a container called a Downs cell. The sodium chloride is first mixed with calcium chloride to lower the melting temperature to about 600 °C (1100 °F), saving energy and reducing costs. When electricity is passed through molten sodium chloride, it decomposes, or breaks down, to form sodium metal and chlorine gas.

Sodium and titanium

Sodium is used to extract titanium from its ores using the Kroll process, invented by William Kroll in 1932. Titanium is a light but strong metal that does not rust. It is used in the aircraft industry and for the artificial joints used in joint replacement surgery. In the Kroll process, liquid titanium (IV) chloride is heated with sodium or magnesium in an unreactive argon atmosphere. This forms titanium and sodium chloride. The sodium chloride is dissolved in water and washed away, leaving the titanium behind.

The equation for the reaction between titanium (IV) chloride and sodium is

titanium (IV) chloride + sodium → titanium + sodium chloride

$$Ti_2Cl_4 + 4Na \rightarrow 2Ti + 4NaCl$$

Sodium is used as the coolant in some designs for nuclear reactors. This Superphénix reactor near Lyon, France contained 4,500 tons of sodium.

Sodium in nuclear reactors

Power plants use steam to drive turbines, which in turn drive the generators. Nuclear reactors use the heat produced from nuclear reactions to make steam. The heat must be carried out of the reactor by a coolant so it can boil the water. Sodium is often used as a coolant in nuclear reactors because it has a high heat capacity, which means it can store a lot of heat. It also melts into a runny liquid at only 98 °C (208 °F), so it can be pumped through tubes inside the reactor.

Nuclear reactors

The fuel in nuclear reactors usually contains uranium. When a uranium atom splits in a nuclear reaction, it fires off two or three high-speed neutrons. If these neutrons hit other uranium atoms, the atoms split and give off even more neutrons, causing a chain reaction. A huge amount of heat is produced in addition to neutrons and other radiation. Sodium slows down neutrons that whizz around inside the reactor, making them more likely to split uranium atoms.

Sodium must not be allowed to cool down or it will solidify inside the tubes and pumps. It must not be permitted to leak into the air or water, either, because it will react with them and explode.

Sodium Chloride

Sodium chloride is often called table salt or just salt. It is the most common sodium compound, and more than 200 million tons of salt are produced each year.

Salt and salt deposits

Salt, a white solid that forms box-shaped crystals, dissolves easily in water. Each liter or quart of seawater contains on average 26 grams (0.9 ounce). Salt reserves around the world are almost unlimited, and deposits of rock salt are found in many places. The deposits were formed when water in ancient oceans evaporated.

Let them eat salt

Sodium is vital for our muscles, nerves, and other cells to function properly, and salt is the main source of sodium in our diet. A healthy diet easily provides adequate amounts of salt because it is naturally present in food and often added as flavoring. Salt also preserves food by removing water, making it difficult for microorganisms to grow. However, eating too much salt can cause high blood pressure, which can lead to dangerous health problems. Grazing animals often need extra salt in their diet because the plants they eat do not provide enough sodium. Farmers provide salt blocks for their livestock to lick, and they may also mix salt into their food.

▲
This photo shows crystals of common salt, or sodium chloride, viewed through a microscope.

Salt and salaries

Roman soldiers were paid partly with a ration of salt, called the *salarium*. Later, a part of their wages was supposed to be used for buying salt. We get the word *salary* from this.

Gritty roads

One of the major uses for salt is de-icing roads and sidewalks in the winter. Salt lowers the melting point of ice so that it thaws, even when the temperature is below 0 °C (32 °F). It is often mixed with a small amount of grit (crushed rock) to make it easier for tires and shoes to get a good grip on the ground. Gritting the roads is a relatively cheap way to make roads safer in winter, although snow plows are still necessary if snow is on the ground. The problem with using salt in winter is that it damages the steel reinforcing rods in roads and bridges and causes cars and other vehicles to rust more quickly. It also kills the plants on highway medians, but amazingly, seaside plants that can grow in salty conditions have colonized some inland roadsides.

◀ Rock salt is spread on icy roads in winter to melt the ice. This helps to keep the road clear and stops cars and other vehicles from skidding.

The Chlor-Alkali Industry

Although sodium chloride may be best known as a flavoring for food, it is also an important raw material for producing other chemicals. These include hydrogen, chlorine, and an alkali called sodium hydroxide. Not surprisingly, the industry that produces these chemicals is called the chlor-alkali industry.

Electrolysis of brine

Brine is a very concentrated sodium chloride solution, usually produced by solution mining. When electricity is passed through brine, chlorine gas is formed at the positive electrode. Hydrogen gas and a sodium hydroxide solution form directly from the water and sodium ions. It is quite easy to carry out this reaction in the laboratory, but it becomes more complicated on an industrial scale, especially because hydrogen and chlorine react together explosively!

Solution mining

Rock salt can be mined using cutting tools, but it is also extracted using a process called solution mining. Water is pumped down into the salt deposit and dissolves the salt to produce brine. Air is then pumped in, which pushes the brine to the surface through a pipe.

This diagram shows how solution mining works. Underground salt deposits can be over a kilometer deep. After the salt has been removed, old salt caverns may be used to store oil or industrial waste.

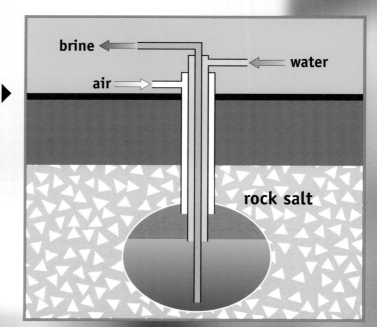

The mercury cell

Throughout the 1900s, the mercury cell was used for the industrial electrolysis of brine. Sodium was prevented from dissolving in water and producing hydrogen at the same time as chlorine by using a layer of mercury as the negative electrode. The sodium dissolved in the mercury instead of in the water to form a mixture of metals, called an amalgam. This was mixed with water later, well away from the chlorine gas. The sodium in the amalgam reacts with the water, producing sodium hydroxide solution and hydrogen gas. Smaller, more efficient devices are now replacing mercury cells.

The membrane cell

The membrane cell, developed in the 1970s, has a positive electrode made from titanium and a negative electrode made from nickel. The hydrogen and chlorine are kept apart by a special layer, called the membrane. The membrane cell uses less electricity than the mercury cell and it is kinder to the environment because it does not use poisonous mercury.

Chlorine and hydrogen

Sodium hydroxide is not the only useful chemical produced by the chlor-alkali industry. Chlorine is used in the manufacture of many products, including PVC plastic, paints, bleach, and chemicals to kill bacteria in swimming pools. Hydrogen is used in the manufacture of margarine and nylon.

▲
Chlorine is one of the important chemicals produced by the chlor-alkali industry. It is used in the manufacture of many products, including chemicals that kill bacteria in swimming pools.

Sodium Hydroxide and More

Forty-five million tons of sodium hydroxide, or caustic soda, as it is known in industry, are produced each year by the electrolysis of brine. It is the cheapest alkali available and widely used in industry to neutralize acids such as the sulfuric acid used in oil refining. It is also an important material for the manufacture of many familiar substances.

Aluminum and soap

Sodium hydroxide is used to purify the aluminum oxide extracted from aluminum ore. Every ton of purified aluminum oxide needs about 100 kilograms (220 pounds) of sodium hydroxide. Just like lithium hydroxide, sodium hydroxide will react with oils and fats to produce compounds such as sodium stearate, used in soap.

Liquid soaps, shampoos, and shower gels contain sodium compounds such as sodium stearate and sodium laureth sulfate. These compounds help to clean dirty skin and hair and make foam.

Paper and artificial fibers

Paper is made from wood, but the wood must be processed to make wood pulp before it can be used. In the kraft process, wood chips are boiled with sodium hydroxide and sodium sulfite, Na_2SO_3. This produces a dark brown pulp that is used to make strong paper grocery bags and cardboard.

Rayon is the oldest synthetic commercial fiber. It is made using cellulose from wood pulp, which is turned into a thick, syrupy substance called viscose, using sodium hydroxide and carbon disulfide. The viscose is sprayed through fine holes into dilute sulfuric acid, which neutralizes the sodium hydroxide and turns the viscose into threads of rayon. Rayon has many uses including clothing, carpets, and bandages. Cellophane wrapping is also made from viscose.

Food and photography

Sodium sulfite and sodium metabisulfite, $Na_2S_2O_5$, are used in the food industry to preserve many foods, including jam, dried fruit, and drinks. In the beer and wine industries, sodium metabisulfite is used to sterilize the equipment before the ingredients are added.

◀ *Dried fruits are often treated with sodium sulfite or sodium metabisulfite, which stops them from turning brown in the air.*

Sodium sulfite and sodium metabisulfite are used in photography to preserve the developing and fixing fluids. In addition, sodium metabisulfite is sometimes used in the stop bath, which halts the developing process. Sodium sulfite is used to produce sodium thiosulfate, $Na_2S_2O_3$, which is sometimes called hypo and is commonly used as a fixer. It reacts with the silver compounds remaining in the film or photographic paper and keeps them from turning dark and spoiling the photograph.

Sodium sulfate

Over 6 million tons of sodium sulfate, Na_2SO_4, are used around the world each year. This compound is found in nature as a mineral called mirabilite and is a byproduct of rayon production and other processes. Sodium sulfate is used to recycle many of the chemicals involved in paper making. Nearly half of it is used as an inexpensive filler in powdered detergents that helps keep the powder dry until use.

Soda Ash

Sodium carbonate, Na_2CO_3, is often called soda ash by the chemical industry. It is found in a mineral called trona and the world's biggest deposit is in Wyoming. Alternatively, sodium carbonate can be made using the Solvay process. It is an important chemical and over 30 million tons of it are produced each year.

The Solvay process

The Solvay process was invented in 1865 by the Belgian chemist Ernest Solvay. There are several complex steps, one of which involves producing sodium bicarbonate by reacting several compounds. When the sodium bicarbonate is heated, it breaks down to form sodium carbonate:

$$\text{sodium hydrogen carbonate} \xrightarrow{\text{heat}} \text{sodium carbonate} + \text{carbon dioxide} + \text{water}$$

$$2NaHCO_3 \longrightarrow Na_2CO_3 + CO_2 + H_2O$$

Glass making

To make glass, sand has to be melted. Sodium carbonate is added to reduce the melting temperature by half, to 800 °C (1500 °F). Unfortunately, because the glass contains sodium carbonate, it dissolves in water! To prevent this, calcium carbonate and magnesium carbonate are added to the glass while it is molten. Ordinary bottle glass, or soda-lime glass, is made in this way. It takes ver 200 kilograms (440 pounds) of sodium carbonate to make each ton of glass, and half of all the sodium carbonate produced is used in this way.

Washing soda

Sodium carbonate is used in household cleaning products and can be bought as washing soda. It produces an alkaline solution when dissolved in water. Sodium carbonate bleaches cotton and removes greasy stains, but it also irritates skin so rubber gloves should be worn while using it.

Sodium bicarbonate

Sodium bicarbonate, $NaHCO_3$, is also called baking soda. It dissolves in water to make a weak alkaline solution and produces carbon dioxide gas if heated or mixed with acids. Baking powder and self-rising flour contain sodium bicarbonate and a dry acid such as tartaric acid. These compounds react when mixed into cake batter, and the carbon dioxide produced helps the cake to rise as it is baked.

Our stomachs produce hydrochloric acid to help digest our food, but if it makes too much we get indigestion. A drink of water containing some sodium bicarbonate helps by neutralizing these acids. Bacteria in the mouth produce acids that can damage teeth, so some toothpastes contain sodium bicarbonate, which works in the same way.

The equation for the reaction between sodium bicarbonate and hydrochloric acid is

sodium bicarbonate + hydrochloric acid → sodium chloride + water + carbon dioxide

$$NaHCO_3 + HCl \rightarrow NaCl + H_2O + CO_2$$

One type of fire extinguisher uses the reaction between sodium bicarbonate and sulfuric acid to produce carbon dioxide gas. This forces water out of the extinguisher and onto the flames.

◀ *These glass bottles are being made in a glass factory. Air is blown into molten glass in a mold to form the shape of the bottle.*

Potassium

Potassium is very similar to lithium and sodium because it is a soft, silvery metal. It reacts fairly vigorously with air and water, so it is also stored in oil.

The discovery of potassium

People have used potassium compounds for thousands of years, mainly for their alkaline properties, but it is never found as a pure metal because it is too reactive. It was not until 1807 that Sir Humphry Davy discovered potassium by passing electricity through molten caustic potash, or potassium hydroxide. To do this he used the battery invented by Alessandro Volta just eight years earlier. Apparently he was so thrilled when he saw silvery potassium metal forming at the negative electrode and bursting into flames that he danced around his laboratory!

The symbol for potassium, K, comes from *kalium,* the Latin word for alkali. Potassium gets its name from potash—the ashes from a pot! People used the ashes from burned wood to make soap. They boiled the ashes in a pot with water, which released the alkalis from them. Then they boiled animal fats with the alkalis to make soap.

▼ *This digging machine is scraping minerals containing potassium compounds from the roof of a potash mine.*

Ashes and alkalis

People have made alkalis for thousands of years by boiling the ashes from plants in water. The word *alkali* comes from the Arabic words *al-qali,* which means "the ash."

Potassium minerals

Potassium is the seventh most abundant element in the earth's crust. On average, each ton of rock contains about 15 kilograms (33 pounds) of potassium in various compounds, including sylvite and carnallite. Both of these compounds contain potassium chloride. Seawater also contains potassium chloride, but in quantities 28 times less than sodium chloride.

The word *potash* is often used to describe potassium oxide, but in the minerals industry this term is used for potassium minerals in general.

◀ *On average, each liter or quart of seawater contains 10.7 grams (0.38 ounce) of dissolved sodium and 0.38 grams (0.01 ounce) of dissolved potassium. Seawater from Wormly, in southern England, is used as the international standard for seawater composition.*

Extraction of potassium

Unlike sodium, which can be produced from sodium chloride using electrolysis, potassium cannot be extracted from potassium chloride this way. This is because potassium chloride has a high melting point, which would make the process expensive. In addition, any potassium produced would just dissolve in the molten potassium chloride. Instead, potassium chloride is heated with sodium. Under normal circumstances there would not be a reaction because sodium is less reactive than potassium. However, the conditions are carefully adjusted so that a small amount of potassium vapor is produced, which is cooled and solidified.

Uses of Potassium

Potassium metal itself has very few uses. At room temperature potassium and sodium are both solid, but a mixture of 78 percent potassium and 22 percent sodium is liquid. This unusual alloy is used as an industrial catalyst and as a cooling fluid in some nuclear reactors.

Radioactive potassium

Radioactive potassium is used as a tracer in medicine. Tracers are chemicals injected into the body to help doctors diagnose illness. Doctors can study where radioactive tracers go by detecting the radiation they produce. Only tiny amounts are needed. Potassium-42 is a radioactive isotope used by doctors to find out how much potassium there is in a patient's bloodstream. It is also used to study the heart and the flow of blood through it. Potassium-42 decays or breaks down very quickly to form an isotope of calcium that is not radioactive.

Isotopes

All atoms of a particular element have the same number of protons and electrons, but different isotopes of an element have different numbers of neutrons. This gives them a different mass number. The most abundant isotope of potassium is potassium-39. Its nucleus contains nineteen protons and twenty neutrons. Potassium-42 has three more neutrons in its nucleus.

Potassium-argon dating

The ages of rocks can be calculated accurately using a method called potassium-argon dating. Rocks usually contain potassium compounds, and some of the potassium will be a radioactive isotope called potassium-40.

This is the fossil of a trilobite, a sea creature that lived about 380 million years ago. The age of the fossil can be determined using potassium-argon dating.

Potassium-40 has a half-life of over a billion years, decaying very slowly to form argon-40. Geologists determine the age of a rock by comparing the amounts of these two isotopes. Young rocks have more potassium-40 than argon-40, and older rocks have more argon-40 than potassium-40.

Half-life

If we study many atoms, we cannot say when an individual atom will decay, but we can predict the time it takes for half of them to decay. This time is called its half-life. Potassium-39 does not seem to decay at all, while other isotopes, such as potassium-40, decay very slowly. Potassium-49 decays extremely quickly, wtih a half-life of just 1.25 seconds.

Potassium superoxide

Potassium metal is used to produce a yellow compound called potassium superoxide, KO_2. This is used in emergency breathing apparatuses because it releases oxygen when it reacts with carbon dioxide or water. Bulky air cylinders are not needed, and the apparatuses can be put on quickly in an emergency.

◀ *This scuba diver is using a rebreather. This type of breathing apparatus converts used air into breathable air.*

The equations for the reactions with potassium superoxide in the breathing apparatus are

potassium superoxide + carbon dioxide → potassium carbonate + oxygen

$$4KO_2 + 2CO_2 \rightarrow 2K_2CO_3 + 3O_2$$

potassium superoxide + water → potassium hydroxide + oxygen

$$4KO_2 + 2H_2O \rightarrow 4KOH + 3O_2$$

Potassium Compounds

Most potassium compounds will dissolve in water, like most sodium compounds, and can be used in all sorts of situations.

Drain cleaner and soap

Potassium hydroxide dissolves in water to produce a strongly alkaline solution, that can react with oils and fats. This makes it a very useful ingredient for drain cleaners. When drains become blocked, the blockage usually contains grease from household waste. The potassium hydroxide in the drain cleaner reacts with the grease, turning it into a soapy mixture that dissolves in water, helping to clear the drain.

Soap can be made by boiling potassium hydroxide solution with vegetable oils, such as palm oil. Different oils produce a variety of compounds, which can be blended together in different amounts to make a wide range of soaps. Potassium hydroxide is also used in the manufacture of potassium phosphate, an ingredient in liquid detergents and artificial fertilizers.

Fertilizers

Plants need elements such as nitrogen, phosphorus, and potassium to grow properly. Potassium helps them produce healthy shoots and leaves, making them resistant to disease. If there is insufficient potassium in the soil, plants suffer from potassium deficiency. Abnormally short stems and leaves that curl and turn yellow are symptoms of this. Farmers add fertilizers to the soil to prevent this from happening. These fertilizers contain compounds such as potassium sulfate and potassium chloride. Potassium nitrate is particularly useful as a fertilizer because it provides plants with nitrogen as well as potassium.

Food and teeth

Potassium nitrate (with sodium nitrate) is used to preserve processed foods, such as bacon and sausages. It is also the active ingredient in most types of toothpaste used for sensitive teeth. Potassium nitrate is also a powerful oxidizing agent used in matches and gunpowder.

Oxidizing agents

Many substances react slowly with the oxygen in air. However, if the temperature is high enough they may catch fire and burn. If we want something to burn really quickly or to burn where there is no air, as in space, we need to supply extra oxygen. Chemicals called oxidizing agents, including potassium nitrate (KNO_3), can supply this extra oxygen.

Matches and fireworks

The potassium nitrate in a match head helps to light the match and enables the chemicals in gunpowder to burn quickly enough to cause an explosion. Potassium chlorate, $KClO_3$, is another powerful oxidizing agent used in matches and explosives, especially in fireworks.

▲
Match heads contain potassium chlorate, phosphorus sulfide, and powdered glass. When a match head is run across a rough surface, the heat from the friction causes it to burst into flame.

LIBRARY
EDWARD LITTLE HIGH SCHOOL

Potassium, Sodium, and Our Bodies

Potassium and sodium are both very important for cells in our bodies to work properly. They are needed to keep the different chemicals in our cells at the right concentration. Potassium ions are the most abundant metal ions inside cells, just as sodium ions are the most plentiful ions outside them. Cells even use energy to keep these two metals in balance.

The sodium-potassium pump

Cells use energy to move sodium out and potassium in. The energy comes from chemical bonds in a compound called adenosine triphosphate, or ATP. The pump is a protein in the cell membrane, which sticks to sodium and potassium ions and moves them in or out of the cell. For every molecule of ATP supplying energy to the pump, three sodium ions move out of the cell and two potassium ions move in.

Potassium and sodium in the diet

Potassium and sodium are needed for our nerves, heart, and muscles to function. A normal diet should provide enough potassium to keep us healthy. Foods that are rich in potassium include bananas, oranges, meat, potatoes, and green vegetables. Salt is found in most foods. In fact salt is added to most processed foods to make them taste better. We are unlikely to suffer from sodium deficiency.

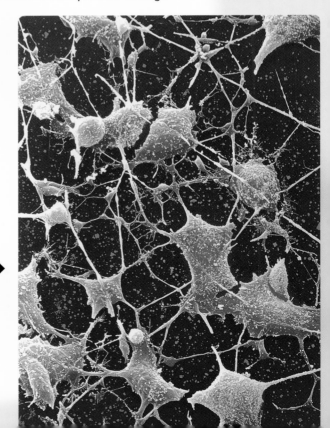

These are nerve cells viewed through an electron microscope. Information is passed between them using electrical nerve impulses, which need sodium and potassium ions to work. ▶

46

Low salt

Too much salt in our diet can lead to high blood pressure, which can cause heart disease and strokes. People suffering from high blood pressure are usually advised by their doctor to reduce their intake of salt. Choosing foods that contain less added salt can help. Also available are salt substitutes, in which two-thirds of the sodium chloride is replaced with potassium chloride.

Rehydration salts

Patients who have lost a lot of body fluids may be given an intravenous drip to replace the lost water and salt. This is a bag containing sterile sodium chloride solution, which is slowly added to the patient's bloodstream through a vein.

Travelers may suffer from diarrhea and lose a lot of water as a result. They can also lose a lot of sodium and potassium,

which is dangerous and even fatal if left untreated. In developing countries more than 4 million children a year died from untreated diarrhea in the 1970s. By the start of the 21st century, the death rate had been reduced by nearly three-quarters because of a simple mixture, called oral rehydration salts, or ORS, dissolved in water. Treatment with ORS is really important in countries where there are few hospitals.

▲
A nurse prepares an intravenous drip containing sterile sodium chloride solution, which is added slowly through a vein into the patient's bloodstream to replace lost body fluids.

A recipe for ORS	
sodium chloride	2.6g
potassium chloride	1.5g
sodium citrate	2.9g
glucose	13.5g
water	1 liter

Rubidium

Rubidium is a soft, silvery metal that reacts so quickly with air and water that it must be stored in unreactive argon gas. Rubidium melts at 39 °C (102 °F) and may become liquid on an extremely hot day.

The discovery of rubidium

Rubidium was discovered in 1861 by two German chemists, Gustav Kirchhoff and Robert Bunsen, while using a spectroscope to study the light emitted by the mineral lepidolite in a flame test. They named the new element rubidium, after the Latin word for dark red because its spectrum contains two dark red lines.

Extraction of rubidium

Rubidium is the sixteenth most abundant element in the Earth's crust even though each ton of rock only contains about 60 grams (2 ounces). Small amounts of it occur in various minerals, including pollucite, carnallite, and lepidolite. Rubidium is usually obtained from the materials left over after the extraction of lithium from lepidolite. Several complex steps are needed to separate rubidium from the other elements in the waste material, which makes rubidium a relatively expensive metal.

Uses of rubidium

Rubidium is not only expensive, it is also difficult to handle safely because of its reactivity. Even some of its compounds can be hazardous. Rubidium is used to remove traces of air in some vacuum tubes. These electronic devices are now only used in expensive stereo systems, professional guitar amplifiers, and the radio transmitters used by radio stations to broadcast their programs. They were more widely used before the transistor was invented in 1947 and semiconductors took over. To make a vacuum inside the vacuum tube, most of the air is removed from it at the factory using a pump. Then a small amount of reactive metal is put inside each tube before it is sealed. The metal is called a getter because it gets any remaining air by reacting with it, producing a really good vacuum.

Rubidium is used in some designs of photoelectric cells. When light shines on them, a small electric current is produced. The current stops if the light is removed. Rubidium can be made to give off electrons when light hits it, so it is used in the negative electrode of these devices. Photoelectric cells are used in situations where a beam of light falling on them could be blocked. These include automatic doors in elevators and devices that count objects moving along conveyor belts in factories.

▼ *Vacuum tubes are electronic devices used in radio transmitters, some stereo systems, and guitar amplifiers. Rubidium is one of the reactive metals used to remove traces of air from inside vacuum tubes.*

Cesium

Cesium is a very soft metal with a faint gold color. It reacts so quickly with air and water that it must be stored in a vacuum or argon gas. Cesium melts at 28 °C (82 °F) and may turn into a very runny liquid if you hold its container.

The discovery of cesium

Gustav Kirchhoff and Robert Bunsen (below) discovered cesium in 1860, a year before they discovered rubidium. Cesium was named after the Latin word for "sky blue" because its spectrum contains two blue lines.

Working with Gustav Kirchhoff, Robert Wilhelm Bunsen (1811–1899), right, examined the spectrum of light given off by the Sun and was able to identify the elements in the Sun. They discovered cesium in 1860 and rubidium in 1861.

Extraction of cesium

Cesium is quite rare in Earth's crust and, on average, each ton of rock contains just 2 grams (0.07 ounce) of it. Like the other alkali metals, cesium never occurs naturally as a pure metal. Pollucite (cesium aluminum silicate) is a good source of cesium. It is also found in small amounts in other minerals, such as lepidolite and can be extracted from the materials left over from lithium production. Several complex steps are needed to isolate cesium from other elements, especially rubidium, which is very similar chemically. One method involves purifying the cesium compounds and converting them into cesium cyanide. This is then melted and broken down to form cesium by passing electricity through it.

Into space with cesium

Like rubidium, cesium is used as a getter in vacuum tubes. However, in the 20th century it was involved in something far more exciting—developing engines for spacecraft.

Engines called ion drives are often mentioned in science fiction films, but now they actually exist. In an ordinary rocket engine, burning fuel produces hot gases that shoot out of the end of the rocket. These gases push the spacecraft into space and on to other planets. Ion engines work differently and are smaller and more efficient. High-speed electrons bombard the atoms in the fuel and cause them to lose some of their own electrons. The atoms become positively charged particles called ions, and a powerful electric field accelerates them to about 40 kilometers (25 miles) per second. The ions shoot out of the back of the engine and push the spacecraft forward. Unlike ordinary rockets, ion drives remain with the spacecraft for a long time, gradually accelerating the spacecraft to great speeds.

The first ion engines used cesium for their fuel. In 1974, a cesium ion engine was successfully tested on a satellite in space. Unfortunately, during the engine's ground tests tiny amounts of reactive cesium were sprayed everywhere. This was very messy and ion engines now use unreactive xenon gas as a fuel.

Atomic Clocks

The best atomic clocks rely on cesium atoms. Atomic clocks are accurate to about one second in every 20 million years and ensure that clocks all over the world keep in step with on another. Many countries keep their own atomic clocks in national laboratories. They provide accurate time signals, which are important for computer networks such as the Internet to work properly. All sorts of businesses rely on the signals to run smoothly, including television and radio stations and telephone and electric power companies.

The second
The second is the basic unit of time. Because cesium clocks are so accurate, scientists define the second as the amount of time it takes for a cesium-133 atom to vibrate exactly 9,192,631,770 times.

Resonating cesium atoms
When you first learned how to use a swing, it is more than likely that you moved your legs too slowly or too quickly, you used a lot of energy and the swing hardly moved. However once your legs moved at the right speed you probably found that you could swing much higher. This is because more of your energy went into the swing. This is called the resonance frequency. Atoms do not play on swings, but they do have a resonance frequency.

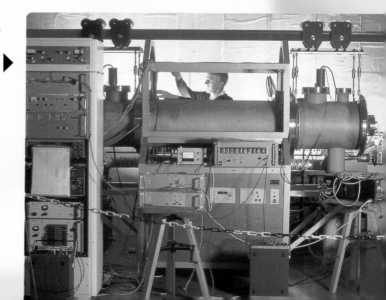

The CS_2 cesium atomic clock at the German National Standards Laboratory, near Hannover. Atomic clocks may not look like ordinary clocks or work like them, but they are incredibly accurate— usually to within at least one second in a million years.

In a cesium atomic clock, cesium is heated to boil off some atoms. These atoms are exposed to microwaves, and they vibrate as a result. The resonance frequency of cesium atoms is 9,192,631,770 vibrations per second, which can be measured very accurately. Electronic devices in the clock lock on to the resonance frequency, kind of like tuning into a favorite radio station, and the signals given off are used to measure time.

Radioactive cesium
When radiation is not controlled, it damages healthy cells, causing cancer and other illnesses. However, managed radioactivity is an effective treatment for some cancers and radioactive cesium may be used in machines for this purpose.

Radiotherapy
A teletherapy machine contains a radioactive isotope such as cesium-137. Cesium-137, which does not occur naturally, is radioactive and has a half-life of 30 years. A beam of radiation from the teletherapy machine is aimed at the cancerous growth, damaging and killing the cells. This device treats some cancers very successfully.

The Goiânia accident
Goiânia is a city 180 kilometers (110 miles) southwest of the Brazilian capital, Brasília. In 1987, hundreds of people in Goiânia were accidentally exposed to radiation from cesium chloride that contained radioactive cesium-137. Men looking for scrap metal to sell broke into an old hospital and took apart an abandoned teletherapy machine. They found a white powder inside that sparkled and glowed blue in the dark. This was radioactive cesium chloride. They passed the compound around to friends and relatives to look at. No one realized how dangerous it was until people began to fall ill. Four people, including a child, eventually died, and some contaminated houses had to be demolished. Brazil has changed the regulations that concern the disposal of radioactive materials to avoid anything like this happening again.

Cesium Compounds

Cesium hydroxide is the strongest known alkali and will even react with glass. However it is used as a catalyst for some chemical reactions. Other cesium compounds are far less reactive, such as cesium chloride, which biochemists use to separate pieces of DNA with the help of a centrifuge.

Cesium azide

It is difficult to handle cesium safely because it melts easily and is very reactive. Cesium is often supplied as a compound of cesium and nitrogen, called cesium azide, CsN_3. This is a colorless solid that breaks down when heated to form cesium and nitrogen gas.

Centrifuges and cesium chloride

If water and sand grains are mixed together in a test tube, gravity pulls the sand to the bottom quickly. If powdered sand is used instead, it sinks very slowly because the particles are so small. Centrifuges help small particles like cells sink quickly. The test tubes are spun around and around at high speed, and the particles are flung to the bottom very rapidly.

▼ *Centrifuges are used to separate the different components of blood and other substances. Plastic or glass tubes are loaded onto a rotor inside the centrifuge and then spun around very quickly.*

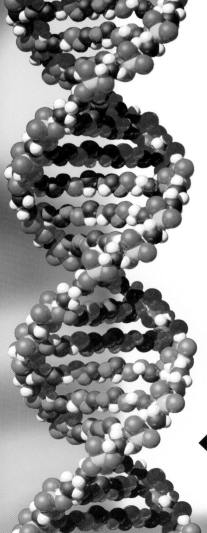

Ultracentrifuges

Small tabletop centrifuges can spin at around 6000 rpm (revolutions per minute). They produce forces of around 3,000 x g—3,000 times the force of gravity. Ultracentrifuges spin even faster than this and produce huge forces of 350,000 x g or more.

Solutions of cesium chloride are very dense. When spun in an ultracentrifuge, the cesium in the cesium chloride is pulled toward the bottom of the test tube. This makes the solution very dense at the bottom and less dense at the top.

DNA is a long, complex chemical that carries the genetic information in cells. Biochemists often need to separate pieces of DNA for their research. Fortunately, the DNA pieces all have different densities, which allows them to be separated using a centrifuge. Once in the ultracentrifuge, the DNA pieces are pulled toward the bottom of the test tube until each one reaches a part of the cesium chloride solution that has a matching density, where it remains. The layers of DNA formed in this way are easily removed when the ultracentrifuge stops.

Infrared spectrometers

Crystals of cesium bromide or cesium iodide are used to make the windows in infrared spectrometers because infrared light passes easily through them. Chemists use these machines to analyze samples of their chemicals. Each chemical absorbs infrared light differently. The spectrometer measures how a beam of infrared light is changed as it passes through a sample, and every chemical has a unique fingerprint of results.

◄ *A model of a section of DNA, or deoxyribonucleic acid, showing the famous double helix spiral structure discovered by James Watson, Francis Crick, and Rosalind Franklin in 1953.*

Francium

Francium is an extremely rare, radioactive metal that no one has seen enough of to know what it looks like. Chemists can use the periodic table to predict its properties. It is likely to be extremely reactive because elements in group 1 become more reactive from top to bottom, and francium is at the bottom of the group. It would probably explode into flames if it came in contact with air and water and would need to be stored in a vacuum.

The discovery of francium

When Dimitri Mendeleev developed his periodic table, he realized not all the elements had been discovered. Mendeleev confidentally left gaps in his table, ready to receive the missing elements. This allowed chemists to predict the likely properties of the missing elements by studying those positioned around the gaps. It also gave them strong hints about which minerals might contain the missing elements. One of the gaps was for eka-cesium, which he expected would be located immediately below cesium. Francium, the missing eka-cesium, was discovered in 1939 by the French chemist Marguerite Perey who named the new element after her native country.

Marguerite Perey (1909–1975) discovered ▶
francium while working as a technician at
the Curie Institute, in Paris. She later
became the first woman member of the
French Academy of Sciences.

Production of francium

Francium is very radioactive. It is formed when actinium, present in uranium ores, gives off radiation. Francium-223, its most abundant isotope, has a half-life of only 22 minutes and decays to form astatine and radium. This means that if you could manage to get a gram of it, after four hours there would be less than half a milligram left! This is why there are probably only a few grams of francium in Earth's crust at any one time.

Modern alchemy

Ancient alchemists tried in vain to convert lead into gold. They failed because a nuclear reaction is required to convert one element into another—chemical reactions just cannot do it. To get a new artificial element with a bigger nucleus, a machine called a particle accelerator is used to accelerate ions to tremendously high speeds. These are fired into a metal target, and if the scientists are lucky an atom and an ion stick will together to make a new atom that has a much larger nucleus.

Francium has no uses apart from scientific research. Scientists even have to make their own francium using nuclear reactions if they want to study it. One way to do this is to bombard gold with oxygen ions in a machine called a particle accelerator.

▼ *The inside of Linac, a particle accelerator at the Fermi National Accelerator Laboratory (Fermilab), near Chicago. Powerful electric fields accelerate particles such as protons to very high speeds.*

Find Out More About the Alkali Metals

Some useful information about the alkali metals

Element	Symbol	Atomic number	Melting point (°C)	Boiling point (°C)	State at 25°C	Density at 25°C (g/cm³)
lithium	Li	3	181	1327	solid	0.53
sodium	Na	11	98	883	solid	0.97
potassium	K	19	64	757	solid	0.86
rubidium	Rb	37	39	688	solid	1.53
cesium	Cs	55	28	678	solid	1.87
francium	Fr	87	not known	not known	probably solid	not known

Compounds

These tables show you the chemical formulas of most of the **compounds** mentioned in this book. For example, sodium sulfate has the formula Na_2SO_4. This means it is made from two sodium **atoms**, one sulfur atom, and four oxygen atoms, joined together by chemical **bonds**.

Lithium compounds

Lithium compound	formula
amblygonite	$LiAlFPO_4$
lepidolite	$KLi_2AlSi_4O_{10}(OH)F$
petalite	$LiAlSi_4O_{10}$
spodumene	$LiAlSi_2O_6$
lithium bromide	$LiBr$
lithium carbonate	Li_2CO_3
lithium chloride	$LiCl$
lithium fluoride	LiF
lithium hydroxide	$LiOH$
lithium oxide	Li_2O
lithium sulfate	Li_2SO_4

Sodium compound	formula
cryolite	Na_3AlF_6
halite	$NaCl$
sodium nitrate	$NaNO_3$
sodalite	$Na_8Al_6Si_6O_{24}Cl_2$
trona	$Na_3(HCO_3)(CO_3)$
sodium carbonate	Na_2CO_3
sodium chloride	$NaCl$
sodium citrate	$Na_3C_6H_5O_7$
sodium bicarbonate	$NaHCO_3$
sodium hydroxide	$NaOH$
sodium metabisulfite	$Na_2S_2O_5$
sodium stearate	$C_{17}H_{35}COONa$
sodium sulfate	Na_2SO_4
sodium sulfite	Na_2SO_3
sodium thiosulfate	$Na_2S_2O_3$

Sodium compounds

Potassium compound	formula
carnallite	$KCl.MgCl_2$
sylvite	KCl
potassium carbonate	K_2CO_3
potassium chlorate	$KClO_3$
potassium chloride	KCl
potassium hydroxide	KOH
potassium nitrate	KNO_3
potassium oxide	K_2O
potassium sulfate	K_2SO_4
potassium superoxide	KO_2

Potassium compounds

Rubidium compound	formula
rubidium superoxide	RbO_2

Rubidium compounds

Find Out More (continued)

Cesium compounds

Cesium compound	formula
pollucite	$(CsNa)_2Al_2Si_4O_{12}$
cesium azide	CsN_3
cesium bromide	$CsBr$
cesium chloride	$CsCl$
cesium cyanide	$CsCN$
cesium hydroxide	$CsOH$
cesium iodide	CsI
cesium superoxide	CsO_2

Acids

Acid compound	formula
hydrochloric acid	HCl
nitric acid	HNO_3
sulfuric acid	H_2SO_4

Other compounds

Other compound	formula
ammonia	NH_3
calcium carbonate	$CaCO_3$
carbon dioxide	CO_2
carbon disulfide	CS_2
hydrogen chloride	HCl
magnesium carbonate	$MgCO_3$
tartaric acid	$C_4H_6O_6$
titanium (IV) chloride	$TiCl_4$
water	H_2O

Glossary

alloy mixture of two or more metals, or a mixture of a metal and a nonmetal

alkali liquid with a pH above 7. When a base dissolves in water, it makes an alkaline solution.

atom smallest particle of an element that has the properties of that element

atomic number number of protons in the nucleus of an atom

bond force that joins atoms together

catalyst substance that speeds up reactions without getting used up

compound substance made from the atoms of two or more elements, joined together by chemical bonds

decay process in which the nucleus of a radioactive substance breaks up, giving off radiation and becoming the nucleus of another element

density mass of a substance compared to its volume (how much space it takes up). To find the density or a substance, you divide its mass by its volume.

DNA (deoxyribonucleic acid) long, complex chemical that carries the genetic information and is the substance of inheritance for almost all living things

electrolysis breaking down a compound by passing electricity through it.

electron particle in an atom that has a negative electric charge. Electrons are found in shells around the nucleus of an atom.

element substance made from only one type of atom

extract to remove a chemical from a mixture of chemicals

fertilizer chemical that give plants the elements they need for healthy growth

filler substance added to a product to improve its properties

group vertical column of elements in the periodic table. Elements in a group have similar properties.

half-life time taken for half the atoms of a radioactive substance to decay

ion charged particle made when atoms lose or gain electrons

isotope atoms of an element with the same number of protons and electrons, but a different number of neutrons

mass number number of an atom's protons added to the number of its neutrons

mineral substance that is found naturally but does not come from animals or plants. Metal ores and limestone are examples of minerals.

molecule smallest particle of a compound that exists by itself. A molecule is made from two or more atoms joined together.

neutralize when an acid and an alkali or base react together. The resulting solution is neutral, which means it is not acidic or alkaline.

neutron particle in an atom's nucleus that does not have an electric charge

nuclear reaction reaction involving the nucleus of an atom. Radiation is produced in nuclear reactions.

nucleus center part of an atom that has a positive electric charge.

ore mineral from which metals can be taken out and purified

oxidizing agent chemical that can add oxygen to other chemicals or remove electrons from them

period horizontal row of elements in the periodic table

periodic table chart in which all the known elements are arranged into groups and periods

prism block of transparent material, usually glass, that has a triangular cross-section

proton particle in a atom's nucleus that has a positive electric charge

radioactive producing radiation

radiation energy or particles given off when an atom decays

reaction chemical change that produces new substances

refining removing impurities from a substance to make it more pure. It can also mean separating the different substances in a mixture, for example, in oil refining

spectroscope piece of equipment that splits the light given off by something into its spectrum

spectrum all the different colors that make up a ray of light

subatomic particle particle smaller than an atom, such as a proton, neutron, or electron

vacuum empty space containing very little air or none at all

welding joining two or more metals together, usually by heating them

Timeline

potassium discovered	1807	Sir Humphry Davy
sodium discovered	1807	Sir Humphry Davy
lithium discovered	1817	Johann Arfvedsen
cesium discovered	1860	Gustav Kirchhoff and Robert Bunsen
rubidium discovered	1861	Gustav Kirchhoff and Robert Bunsen
francium discovered	1939	Marguerite Perey

Further Reading and Useful Websites

Books
Oxlade, Chris. *Acids and Bases* Chicago: Heinemann Library, 2002.

Oxlade, Chris. *Metals*. Chicago: Heinemann Library, 2002.

Websites
WebElements™
http://www.webelements.com
An interactive periodic table crammed with information and photographs.

Proton Don
http://www.funbrain.com/periodic
The fun periodic table quiz!

Mineralogy Database
http://www.webmineral.com
Useful information about minerals, including color photographs and information about their chemistry.

DiscoverySchool
http://school.discovery.com/clipart
Help for science projects and homework and free science clip art.

Creative Chemistry
http://www.creative-chemistry.org.uk
An interactive chemistry site with fun practical activities, quizzes, puzzles and more.

Index